AF221271

Miku Kumiko

nonsense
ナンセンス

koans

meditations

thoughts

remarks

nonsense

Bibliografische Information der Deutschen
Nationalbibliothek: Die Deutsche
Nationalbibliothek verzeichnet diese Publikation in
der Deutschen Nationalbibliografie; detaillierte
bibliografische Daten sind im Internet
über dnb.dnb.de abrufbar.

Herstellung und Verlag:

BoD – Books on Demand, Norderstedt

ISBN: 9783753424224

Part 1

See

We went away to take a closer look

(Balanced)

A little more precise

More

We get enough for free and dare even more

(Twisted)

Get more

Nothing

All days are used up quickly and nothing
comes from anything

(Wasted)

Become nothing

Begin

Finished thoughts can always start over

(Believed)

Thoughts begin

Stay

Fled and left without talents

(Succeeded)

Remain fled

Give

Hopefully you want to give me your
unconditional attention

(Faith)

Without attention

Greater

Torn joys don't make my happiness any
greater

(Hope)

Make luck

Waning

It all made sense at first, then run away and
disappear

(The End)

Initially waning

Love

The end is transparent without truth and
without hate and without love

(Beginning)

Without love

To lose

Called thoughts do not dare to express
themselves and slowly lose the day

(Thought out)

To dare

Sense

The greatest messages do not shine in the
heart and cloud the mind

(Size)

Meaning shine

To notice

Occasionally lie and today I don't notice

(Freedom)

Occasionally notice

Self

Throw yourself down and watch yourself

(Humility)

Throw yourself

On it

The heart can like to be wounded and you
don't think about it

(Joy)

May be

Free

The sacrifice will not get you anywhere and
you will finally be free

(Reverie)

Continue free

You

Pain attacks you and beautifies you

(Maturity)

Embellish pain

Be

Spend the day artfully and be alone in the
evening

(Successful)

Be artistic

Be

Hopefully well criticized and yet not seen

(Vain)

Be hopeful

Prescribe

Did not find any resting points and dictate the
day

(Thoughts)

Prescribe resting points

Handle

Think about yesterday and redefine the
meaning

(Nonsense)

Grab yesterday

To get

I can't get rid of the intrusive thoughts and I
almost get out of breath

(Died)

Get thoughts

To have

In the end, think back and you still get nothing

(Freedom)

Do not have anything

Feeling

Let go of the pain and feel it even more

(Believed)

Feel pain

To hope

Always think of a new life and hope for a nice meaning

(Futureless)

Hope for life

Nothing

The meaning comes to an end without a
thought and you dissolve

(Thought out)

Meaning disappears

Alone

Angry people kill your imaginary life and you
are alone again

(Disgusting)

People killed

Stay

Do you want to be good and still don't want
to stay here?

(Unseen)

Be good

Turn

Better your life and make a pointless turn

(Renew)

Turn better

Lost

What I heard was lost between many thoughts
and lost forever

(Touched)

Lost thoughts

Come

Think carefully and make a well-considered
decision

(Regulate)

Come on thoroughly

Thereon

There will never be any extraordinary days
and you may believe in vain

(Exhaled)

Give days

Say

The sense was better and there is almost
nothing left to say

(Rest)

Say meaning

Made

There is nothing more to say and the
beginning has been made

(Infinite)

Don't say anything

Day

Found thoughts don't dare to express
themselves and I lose the day

(Doubt)

Express thoughts

Love

The end is transparent without truth, without
hate, without love

(To die)

Hate is

Say

The feeling is better and there is little to be
said

(Build up)

Better to say

To

The heart likes to hurt and you don't think
about it

(Get lost)

You think

Be

The sacrifice will get you nowhere and you
will finally be free

(Be good)

Be a victim

New

Think about yesterday and re-explain the
meaning

(Heartless)

Rethink

Sense

Always think of a new life and expect a nice
purpose

(Thought out)

Think wisely

Nothing

The meaning ends without thinking and you
disappear into a void

(Freedom)

Nothing ends

Not

The best message shines in your heart and
does not cloud your heart

(Enlightenment)

And seems

Be

An angry person kills your imaginary life and you will be alone again

(Masterful)

Be a person

Made

There is nothing to be said and it has started

(Once again)

Say start

Believe

There is never a special day and you can believe in waste

(Carefully)

Never believe

Give

Hopefully you can give me your unconditional attention

(Flirt)

Hopefully there is

Seen

Hopefully you've been criticized, but I haven't seen myself yet

(Selfishness)

Hopefully seen

At the

I found a breakpoint and didn't specify the day

(Trust)

I gave

See

I will see better

(Find)

To see it

Breath

I cannot get rid of disturbing thoughts and I
am out of breath

(Get lost)

Get rid of thoughts

Left

I want to get better, but there's no one left

(Displace)

Nobody stays

Happens

Every day is used quickly and nothing
happens

(To have)

Nothing used

More

Let go of the pain and feel it even more

(Path)

Feel more

Talent

Run away and go without talent

(Let go)

Run without it

Not

Sometimes I lie and don't even notice today

(Blinded)

Sometimes not

Turn

Fix your life and make a pointless turn

(Direction)

Do the life

Nothing

In retrospect, there is still nothing

(Carefully)

In retrospect, nothing

You

Pain attacks you and beautifies you

(Misunderstanding)

Embellish pain

Begin

You can always start over with your thoughts

(Trust)

Thoughts begin

Decisions

Think carefully and make well-thought-out
decisions

(Getting lost)

Make decisions

Alone

Spend the day skillfully and be alone in the
evening

(Salvation)

Sent alone

Lost

What I heard was lost through many thoughts
and lost forever

(Chance)

Always thoughts

Self

We get enough for free and hardly trust each
other anymore

(Fear)

We ourselves

At

Throw yourself down and look at you

(Makes)

Begin

Greater

Torn joy doesn't make my happiness any
greater

(Egoism)

No luck

I

Notice first that I am running fast and now I
am sinking

(Selfless)

Me first

Slowly

You don't dare to express the said comments
and the day is slowly fading away

(A lot of)

Slowly faded

Love

The end is transparent, there is no truth, no
hate, no love

(Arrived)

End there

Say

I feel good and have little to say

(Blurred)

Feel little

To

You like to hurt your heart and not think about it

(To suffer)

About you

Approved

The victim is nowhere to be found and you will eventually be set free

(Happiness)

Find victims

New

Think about yesterday and redefine the meaning

(Untangled)

Rethink

Aims

Always think about a new life and set big goals for yourself

(Spoiled)

Think goals

Go away

It ends without thinking and you will never leave

(Hopefully)

Without leaving

Not

The best message shines in your heart and does not cloud your heart

(To shine)

Does not tarnish

Be

Your spiritual life will be destroyed and you
will be lonely again

(Beginning)

Be the life

At the

Nothing started

(The end)

Nothing

Trust

There is never a special day and you can trust
the waste

(Ease)

Never trust

Attention

I look forward to your unconditional attention

(Feelings)

Attention

Seen

You have been criticized but not yet seen

(Let go)

Not criticized

Mentioned

I found a breakpoint and it was not
mentioned that day

(Dependency)

Breakpoint mentioned

Seen

I've seen you many times

(Premonitions)

I saw you

Breath

I can't get rid of annoying thoughts and I'm
out of breath

(To die)

Thoughts can

Left

I want to be good, but there is nobody left

(Arrived)

Left behind

Happens

Use quickly every day and nothing will happen

(Run)

Don't use anything

Feeling

Let go of the pain and let it feel more

(See)

Let feel

Talent

Escape without talent

(Resolution)

Without escaping

I

Sometimes lying

(Accuracy)

I lie

Turn

Adjust your life and make a meaningless turn

(Courage)

Do the life

Rethink

Nothing to think about yet

(Break up)

Rethink

You

Pain hits you and beautifies you

(Accept)

Pain hits

Begin

You can restart at any time

(No chance)

Start anytime

Decisions

Think carefully and make well-thought-out
decisions

(Freeze)

Make decisions

Alone

Spend the day well and be alone in the
evening

(Commute)

Spend the evening

Lost

What I heard was lost in many thoughts and
lost forever

(Movements)

Heard thoughts

Do

We have done enough for free and we have
the courage to do more of it

(Return)

We do it

At

Throw yourself in and look at you

(Encouraged)

To you

More

My happiness is no longer a torn joy

(Thought out)

Joy is

You

First they see they were running fast and now
they are sinking

(Projection)

They ran

Part 2

Darkness

After seeing the plan and thinking carefully
about the day, sentences turn the world
around, just come through and are there.

Wrung out

Well wrung out the construct and collected
the good inventions of life.

Games

Reinvent old games, feel comfortable for a
moment, and talk to yourself.

Rain

The raindrop clings to the pane of glass, the
thoughts cling to life with the raindrop and hit
you.

Illusion

The illusion of knowledge narrows my good
work breaks and I breathe.

Attitude

Fine tones emerge from the noises, and the surroundings become even narrower and the morning sun warms you up.

Reason

A very good reason to live is to know better without getting caught by yourself or by others.

Nose

Aligning with the nose will help get there and die.

Danger

The smell on the fingers opens up a new world and captivates.

Without

Especially the word without has a lot of content and likes to lead us into an innocent world and turn us around.

Useful

Useful things are good to us and must not be lost until the end.

Finally

Finiteness takes us to infinity, let's check the opinions, we just want to adopt them.

Status

The good state of neglected shocks and makes us think, because performance counts and then I can.

Sun

The sun innocently penetrates the sunburn.

Blooming

The old man blossoms for a moment, looks around the happy group and takes the last train home, everything seems to be fine.

Devastate

The fish stinks and the hunger scolds
impatiently.

Buds

Excited, they all run blindly into ruin, take a
short breath and grow old quickly.

Very difficult

Right now you have to be rock hard and
endure a lot of pain so you can get to heaven
and finally be happy.

First

The train started at the beginning, nobody
heard a noise, it had not been so quiet for a
long time, and it was the beginning again.

Unfounded

Forgetting everything and being politely and
unfoundedly accused.

Equipment

To get to the thoughts of others over long distances, to part and slip away.

Sense

If you turn around, a great secret will be buried and will remain unknown.

Hand

Squeeze the enemy's hand without strength and give up life and happiness comes suddenly and creates.

Glass

The breaking glass was in the head, nobody expected the end now.

Food

Swallow the food quickly and be a connoisseur, define and differentiate the claim to be a connoisseur.

Liberation

Going to church out of tiredness and scratchy
thoughts and hope for the final deliverance
after you are well.

Once again

Again and again the good righteous appear
disgustingly unjust.

Extraterrestrial

Not to be at home in the garden, to hope for
an explanation for today in space and to put
all mysticism in the plastic bag.

In time

Wear the right shirt at the right time and
arrive on time for the funeral.

Dreamy

Fly dreamily through the air, breathe in other
people's scents, wash me and be a dreamer of
the best kind.

Heroes

Since I got a medal, I can now call myself a person.

High

The clouds in the sky seem to be flying pretty high, know the past by heart, are a decal and laugh.

Any

For good reasons the driver could not stop, all responsibility lay with the others and love was also a word.

Fast

The bird on the windowsill chirps the morning song far too quickly.

Out

How far you have to go to be high, to play
with life and get more and be higher, you did
well.

Responsibility

I give you the responsibility, it's really none of
my business how you are.

Worm

The worm has found your mind hole and will
find a home here and stay with you for the
rest of your life.

Heart

With an empty heart I meet my heart, with an
empty heart I meet your heart, with an empty
heart I meet being.

Jail

The life in the dream prison completed very
safely.

Love

In the thirst for love, forget the self, think
about being good and ask.

Ask

And we ask and pray, poetry and we are again
in the prison of dreams, in the prison of love.

Morning

A good morning brings hope back, a good day
makes you forget about dying for a moment,
it becomes a good day.

Reborn

To be born again and again, to die again and
again.

Fear

Fear moved you, the good days are not over
yet.

Fear free

Fear or fearlessness, spring will come to you
and me.

Crosses

The two crosses stood on the mountain and
in me, carried more than one cross and lost
hope or the crosses.

Firmly

We hold on to the crosses forever, they also
give a wrong meaning.

Empty

After finally finding the void and suddenly
rediscovering the crosses, they begin to curse
and be determined.

Wound

Don't let the wound of the heart heal, take proper care of the wound and let it all go to the heart, poison and waste.

Unfortunately

Unfortunately, suffering doesn't always make sense, but suffering always makes sense for displacement.

Trust

Trust your thoughts and get a solid picture of it.

Stiffens

The wave hits me and I feel the solid in me, protected and mute.

Volume

The sounding absolute silence hit you briefly and disappeared at the first thought of success.

Discouraged

Turn discouragement into a feeling of success
and be strong and win and kill and finally be
human.

Excited

Excited is not aroused and doesn't come from
anywhere, it has something to do with
irrationality and spontaneous attacks.

Candle

Stand on a candle holder and think of straight
and the candle, think of the incredible
happiness and be straight.

Apple

I found the apple, but it's a little fishy at heart.

Vomit

The vomit of the friendly drunk smells sour
and drives away my love for wholeness and
understanding.

Dandruff

The shoulders full of strands of hair dampen
the feigned superiority.

Brakes

You slow me down with your superiority and
I keep dreaming of large possessions and I
will show you.

On

When the door opened and the great sage
entered, he stumbled silly.

Friendly

Again, be kind and hug and rule the world
worldly.

Died

The big difference at its core shows everyone
that there is no difference at all, we reproduce
and die.

Saying

The good phrase and saying invite you to sit down and fly away.

Balanced

Sit well balanced on the floor and laugh and have lost again, how is it right, when did you find yourself again.

Hoar frost

To be very mature and very rough, to have lost the beginning and to give yourself the task of finding the beginning again.

Burden

The burden pulls deeper and deeper into the earth; the earth is waiting for you.

Sounds

Penetrated by the tones, by the loud and louder tones, and finally thinking and saying something clever.

Exchange

Exchange some things, fluids and thoughts,
feelings and hard knowledge, beliefs and
stubbornness and yourself.

Jumped off

Again and again and then run away or not.

Short

Of course, look briefly and gently into the
sun, although it hurts, give brief, very friendly
praise to the sun.

Network

Fertilizes the thinker to look for explanations
for the correct meaning.

Brutally

To drink the last sip without consideration
and like to be brutal, that is a timelessly good
quality of character.

Promised

Have not promised anything and despite
being aware of the herd make the way to the
centre of the earth, come here and surrender.

Memory

The memories of the memory are slowly
fading, the memory has become old and thin,
it looks emaciated.

Reason

There is no real reason to gain a lot of
knowledge.

There

To be completely beside yourself, definitely
want to be there and be connected.

Happiness

Happiness to be there and in control of the
worlds is a great misfortune.

Assignment

To get a job do it right and be proud as a warrior, you have to be a warrior.

Occur

I appeared and everything happened by chance, the exemplary strong man spat at me.

Wonder

There are no additional miracles; the known ones must be enough.

Frame

The frame has a beautiful frame function, frame hope.

See

I couldn't see the sun luckily and was stupidly happy.

Slowly

Come back to your senses and be a tidy
person, strengthen your arms and flex your
muscles for joy.

Twisted

Too much thought and the imagination
twisted, nodded and confirmed, confirmed
and thought further, well done.

Weekend

Find a weekend, an end of the year and an
end of life, all effortlessly.

Noise

The constant noise in the little head has
become music, a rustling and clattering and
being kind to everyone, being good.

Numbers

You are allowed to pay anything, no bill is left
open, gifts are dangerous and happiness will
be a terrible punishment.

Abbreviation

The abbreviation has become a habit, there is
no such thing as an abbreviation and it was all
in vain.

Calculated

I calculated well, have a clever mind,
calculated and calculated well, and yet made a
fresh start.

Words

There will always be words, words that
describe all of life.

Open

The calm has opened, the unrest comes again
and everything else is everywhere, hardly takes
up any space and opens everything.

Ready

Now, be ready to get the job done and you've
earned the pleasure of doing it every day
without thinking too much.

Nullity

Grab your vanity and get lost, fall down.

To shine

And the head lights up, many believe that they
can get infected.

Love

Love must not be forgotten here, one or the
other love, imaginary love and empty love.